HOW TO FIND YOUR DREAM JOB

*Proven Strategies for Finding & Securing
Your Dream Job Fast*

IAN TODD

Third Edition

© 2015

Third Edition

Copyright © 2015 by Ian Todd Publishing

A man is a success if he gets up in the morning and gets to bed at night, and in between he does what he wants to do.

Bob Dylan

Table Of Contents

INTRODUCTION

Your Dream Job

If you, like so many others in the world, are suffering from job dissatisfaction, you may be thinking it's time to take your career in a new direction. You may be thinking of leaving a job you've worked at for decades and aren't sure just how to make that leap. You may have struggled with discontentment in the course of your working life and feel like it's time to be true to yourself and finally go for that perfect job you've always wanted. Or you may be just starting out in the working world and need some advice on how to get started.

Let's be honest here. Finding a job is tricky. Finding a good job is difficult.

Finding a good job that also gives you job satisfaction *and* happiness is the ultimate goal – very difficult but also very obtainable if you follow proven steps. No shortcuts but easy to follow steps, proven time and time again, to give you the job you desire.

Do not drift through life in a job which does not fulfill you, emotionally or financially. It is simply not worth it. We spend so much of our lives in work that we owe it to ourselves to make this time valuable, passionate and interesting. Thankfully, it is more possible than you think to tie in these values with a high paying career.

"Think big and don't listen to people who tell you it can't be done. Life's too short to think small."

Tim Ferriss

Whatever your background, and whatever your goal is, this guide is committed to proving that you're only a few simple steps away from getting your perfect job. Laid out in direct, easy to follow steps, this text will teach you absolutely everything you need to know; from your first steps in job hunting, to writing a great resume, to invaluable tips on how you can give your best shot at interviews and beyond.

I know, first hand, how job dissatisfaction and periods of unemployment can affect your life. I struggled through twenty years working in an industry that I knew wasn't quite right for me. But, even though I knew I was unhappy, I was too scared to "jump ship". The thing is, I was actually really good at my job. I was well trained, I worked hard, and progressed steadily over the course of two decades achieving a very respectable position.

However, as the years flew by, I starting feeling low and uninspired. I became short tempered, and listless. I knew I wasn't in the right job for me and I wanted to pursue my true passion but I was scared of "throwing it all away". I had worked very hard to get to where I was and wasn't it way too late to change careers anyway?

Initially, I waved away my ill feelings. I kept on working hard and tried to keep my discontentment at bay. I told myself I could always pursue my hobbies outside of work. Surely no one loves their job, I told myself.

After a while though, it all caught up with me. I felt like I was wasting my life. I had to admit that even though I was very good at what I did, I didn't love what I was doing the way my colleagues seemed to. There was something nagging at me. It seemed wrong to spend my whole life doing something I didn't feel passionate about.

When I finally approached my family and friends about how I was feeling, they were unsupportive to say the least.

"You can't give up a job in this economy!" my father scolded.

"But you're so good at what you do! You'll be getting promoted again soon! Why would you stop now?" said my mother.

"What are you going to do?," my friends asked, **"You can't possibly start at the bottom again. Do you realise how much training you'll have to do? You'll have to start from scratch! You must be crazy!"**

Believe me, I heard it all. Maybe I was crazy! Was it crazy to *"start over"* this far in the game?

Well, it may have been. But I didn't care. I knew there was something better out there for me and I deserved to be happy. It might sound like a cliche but you really do only live once, and if "starting over" was what it would take to make me happy, then that's exactly what I was going to do.

I am happy to say that, though it wasn't always easy, (and it took guts of steel!), eventually, by putting my mind to it, I got my perfect job. I took a leap, and worked hard, and eventually it all paid off. I am now so happy, my only regret not doing it sooner! My experience going through this doubt, uncertainty and feeling alone in the process (but getting through to the other side!) prompted me to start my own business helping other people find their dream job, a company I have been happily and successfully operating for 12 years now.

"Trust not what inspires other members of society to choose a career. Trust what inspires you."

The Lazy Person's Guide to Success

My company guides people through this often difficult period but I am not denying for a single second that it is expensive and often out of the financial reach of many people - that is why I have chosen to write this guide and charge less than the price of a cup of coffee for it! I wanted to make this easy to follow basic advice affordable to everyone.

I hate to think that there are people out there working jobs that they don't love. We all deserve to love our lives, and that is why I am committed to helping you through your process.

So whether you are thinking about "jumping ship" or this is your first time on the playing field, it's time to get started on getting that perfect job!

"You are what you do. If you do boring, stupid, monotonous work, chances are you'll end up boring, stupid, and monotonous."

Bob Black

A Checklist For The Perfect Job

All of us desire a rewarding job or career. As the saying goes, *if you love what you do you never work a day in your life*.

Knowing when you have found the perfect job is sometimes confusing - if you can't answer in the yes to the below list on a regular basis then you might want to start looking for a new job or career!

When you wake in the morning you are excited about the day ahead

How do you feel when you wake in the morning? Are you typically excited and enthused to get up in the morning, get your day started, and get work started? You may find this hard to believe right now, but many people really do feel like that. **HONEST!**
When you love your career, the excitement comes naturally. You do no have to force it or try to find ways to actually make your job more thrilling, it just comes as part of the package. **That** is when you know you have the perfect job.

The hours pass by quickly
When you are working, do you find yourself checking the clock every 5 seconds, wishing time would move faster? Or do you feel that there aren't enough hours in your workday and wish you have *more* time to accomplish everything you want?

You happiness is clear to see
Some people walk into work and have a happy air about them, an emotion that tends to rub off on the people around them. These happy people are extremely important to keep in a business, as they

have the ability to change the entire environment of an office space in seconds. Are you one of them? We all have bad days, but if you do not feel this level of happiness on a regular basis then something is very wrong – act on it now.

Your to-do list each day is something that excites you
Every day is different but no matter what tasks lie ahead of you, you're excited and ready to take it on. Tackling your to-do list and being able to fill it with a new collection of to-dos for the next day exhilarates you. (Okay, that's maybe a slight exaggeration, but you get what I mean!) People who love their jobs accept and embrace the day-to-day routine of what they do, knowing that the little things have to be done first to get to the big things.
If your to-do list simply fills you full of dread than again something if very wrong. Life is too short. It is time to find a new job.

You relish the opportunity to take on new projects
Some people dread the thought of a new project – some people are excited by the prospect. You aren't racing the clock or trying to get ahead of others, you simply look forward to the next big project you can tackle, and you work hard on your current projects so you can get to the next ones. That is true job satisfaction.

You enjoy time spent at work
How do you feel about your office / workplace? Really think about it, how does it make you think? Happy? Excited? Fulfilled? Scared? Bored? Depressed?
Not everyone in your life may not understand it, but you actually like being at work. When you're in your element doing what you love, you feel at your best and you are being paid well. If you can answer yes to this, then you have found the perfect job already and you can probably pass this book on to someone else ;)

Optimism

Put yourself in this situation - a deadline is coming fast and your team seems to be lagging. How are you responding to this? Are you the person cheering everyone on and motivating them to get things done? When other people get overwhelmed are you the one that is making the light at the end of the tunnel seem a lot closer than it appears?

Do you have a helpful and genuine relationship with your coworkers?

If you are a worker with a healthy positive outlook on life then coworkers will know that they can come to you for help or questions and that you will always make an honest attempt to assist.

Are you kind and does your genuine nature shines through, which makes people want to work with you? While most may regard their coworkers in a competitive light, you should truly want to help everyone you can – if you are in the right job for you.

Is the success of the company is important to you?

Ask yourself honestly how you feel about the companys goals and successes? Are they important to you? Do you think about them often? Do you envision the goals on your drive home?

Happy in your job – happy in your life

This is a very important point. People who love their jobs are more likely to have fulfilling personal lives outside of work. Whether they're traveling, in a sports league, or lounging at home, their positivity inspires others and magnetically attracts other people toward them. Study after study has shown that people who work in an unfulfilling job (or who are unemployed) have higher divorce numbers and general unhappiness.

If you don't wake up in the morning excited to pick up where you left your work yesterday, you haven't found your calling yet.
Mike Wallace

Part One: Know What You Really Want

At this stage you may be brand new to the working world. Or you may be - as I was - working in a job that you feel underwhelmed by. You may be feeling undervalued at work, under stimulated, or you may even be feeling hopeless or miserable. You may already be at the stage where you know exactly what direction you'd like to take your career or you might still be unsure about what job would suit you.

"The biggest mistake that you can make is to believe that you are working for somebody else...The driving force of a career must come from the individual. Remember: Jobs are owned by the company, you own your career!"

Earl Nightingale

It is important, firstly, to remember that changing careers and direction in life is normal. As we grow and change throughout our lives, our interests, hobbies, circumstances, and motives will naturally grow and change with us. It might take a bit of soul searching to reach a conclusion about what direction is the right one for you to take. In order for you to make an informed decision about your next (or first) step in the career world, there are a few things you will need to keep in mind.

Knowing Your Interests

This may seem obvious but, it might be a good idea to sit down with a piece of paper and a pen and write down some things you enjoy. Whether that be your hobbies or things you like hearing or learning about.

Whether it be a skill or subject you're already very accomplished in or something you've always wanted to learn. Writing things down is a great way to get a picture of who you are and what it is that will make you ultimately happy. Try not to limit yourself during this soul searching process. Nothing is too big or too small to take into consideration. The goal is to ultimately be happy in your career!

Once you have written that list, think hard and write some jobs or career paths related to each interest. Don't worry about obstacles or things that might prohibit you from ever having these jobs. This exercise is really just a way to see how many paths there are for you to choose from. Then you can start narrowing them down and start getting excited about taking your life in a direction that excites you.

Finding the PERFECT job...is a full time job!

Now that you know what you dream job is, you're ready to get stuck in. The first thing you need to remember is that you've got to take your job hunt seriously. You must go at it with full force. This means being willing to invest time and energy in your search. If you are currently unemployed you must think of your job search as your full time job. Don't sit around in your pyjamas for two weeks watching daytime TV and eating nachos! You must be committed to changing your life if you're ever going to succeed in landing your dream job.

That means getting up in the morning, getting dressed, and staying focused. Resist the urge to put things off and procrastinate. You may end up missing a great job opportunity, or worse, you may end up with an extended period of unemployment and that can be detrimental to your energy levels, financial circumstances, AND your self esteem and general outlook on life. Endeavour to keep your focus and motivation up by keeping active and productive.

If you are currently employed and you cannot afford to leave your current job until you have something new lined up, things can be a bit more difficult. Your time may seem like it's already stretched too thin. You may already be juggling your job, your family life, your hobbies, and other commitments. I understand, it is not always easy.

This type of situation can be tricky but it is by no means uncommon nor impossible. In order to make sure you have the time and energy you'll need to land your dream job, you might need to do a little bargaining and borrowing with your time. It might be beneficial to let go of your evening and weekend plans for a while or to ask family or friends to help out with things like the kids, help around the house, or other tasks you may be able to delegate to others. I know it can be difficult to ask for help for a ton of reasons, but remember this is only a short term solution and you will need some extra time on your hands if you're to get what you want out of your working life!

Another little tip is, if you find you're short on time and struggling to get anything accomplished, use every bit of idle time to your advantage. Think of all the time you spend in your life sitting and waiting and use that time to get your smart phone, tablet, or laptop out and make some progress. Now, I know you're saying, "But I don't HAVE any idle time! I'm swamped!" Believe me, I get it, but why not challenge yourself?

* What about the time you spend commuting every day?

* How about your lunch breaks?

* Time spent in waiting rooms?

* Waiting in the car for your kids to get out of school?

* Waiting for a bus?

You get my point! It might take extra energy and a good deal of discipline, but almost everyone can use their time more efficiently and taking your job hunting seriously could make all the difference in the end. Remind yourself, it might be tiring and a bit stressful but this won't last forever. Your hard work *will* pay off!

Be Realistic About What It Takes

No matter what job it is you're after, you will have to take into account what it will take to make it happen. Your perfect job may require some training and/or education in order for you to gain the skills or knowledge you'll need for it. These things may take more time, energy and money and you will have to account for that when making your plans. You might have to study part time while working another job for a while. You may need to gain experience in a certain field before reaching your ultimate goal.

Whatever the job, you will need to have realistic expectations. Being aware of any obstacles that may be in your way is of upmost importance to maintain your focus and motivation and avoid any unforeseen set backs. Take some time to sit down and research anything you may need to take into consideration.

Think about your training, your experience, your wardrobe, how you commute, anything that might financially or otherwise affect the road to your goal. Think about how much time or money you can spare for any supplies, training, etc you may need to undertake and make realistic plans based on all the facts. The more realistic your plans and expectations are, the easier your journey will be and the more equipped you will be in the face of any obstacles.

Ten Things You Can Start Right Now Today!

The recipe for finding the perfect job can be complex, but the best way to start is to get the ingredients correct. Some things take time, something you can begin immediately. See below for a list of ten things you can start today that really will give you the absolute best chance at finding that dream job. These are the building blocks.

Get Clarity

You need to know where you are going. Without real clarity about what you want to do or how to get it, achieving any sense of fulfilment or being in control of your future will be very difficult. Therefore it's vital to work on getting clear about what your central goal is and how to achieve it, breaking it into small steps.

Invest In Yourself

This journey is important – so give yourself time to work it all out. You will need a significant amount of thought, consideration, time and investment in order to make this change smoothly and to make it the right career change. There are many key stages and turning points to consider so take the time to do it, it is unlikely to all happen overnight.

Create An Action Plan To Follow

By itself, knowing what you want will not ensure that you get it. You need to be clear about your plan of action and how to carry out what you have specifically designed for yourself. Get clear achievable and realistic steps in place. Outline it so that it is broken down into steps that you can work through towards that bigger goal.

Focus Your Energy!

Making a change and finding the right role is not always an easy task. It can be tough, tiresome and long. You need to stay really focused and be efficient around where you put your energy and effort to get the outcome you want. Make sure that you are in control of the key elements in your world and are able to drive forward with the career and life of your choosing. You will need perseverance and determination to help. Being smart about how you spend your time is crucial.

Understanding Your Strengths

Get to know yourself better. Identify what your key strengths are. What are you really good at? What do you enjoy that you are also good at? What skills have you learnt? What are you naturally inclined to do and be better at? Make sure that you get right to the core of it. The more you know yourself the more confident you will become and the better you will be at identify the right role for you and projecting yourself in order to get it.

Ignite That Passion

Without real passion for a role – it will be difficult to get. Even if you do get it – you will find it difficult to maintain and grow within and beyond it. What you want here is the right role. This means something that you are truly passionate about. It might take a bit of experimenting to find what 'floats your boat' – but it will be worth it when you have found it.

Know Your Boundaries

Being clear about what works and what doesn't work for you in order to be happy can be groundbreaking. It sounds simple but so many of us do not actually take the time to work it out. In each different work situation – we may have different boundaries. By being clear about what they are and then communicating this clearly to others and staying true to what is important – will make a huge difference. This impacts work and your personal settings.

Manage and Improve Relationships

This is important from all aspects. If you learn to manage your relationships effectively you will be able to control the process and transition. You will be able to manage your exit smoothly from your current or old role. Understanding where your old boss is coming from and the impact you have on him/her – and how you interact could really influence how you leave a job. How you get your next job and keep it may also rely heavily on your ability to manage relationships well.

Use Your Network!

Learn how to network and harness your connections effectively. This does not mean bombarding people you do not know with emails or adding everyone you can find to linkedin. Neither is this picking up as many business cards you can at a networking event and calling that person part of your 'network'. Real networking is about getting to know people. You need to work on identifying and getting to know those who can help you along your way.

Rid Yourself Of Fears and Insecurities

All of us have them at one stage or another. Many of us keep them for years. However, do not let them stop you. If you are afraid – that is ok – just do not let it take over and control what you do or do not do. If something is blocking you from moving forward – take the time and action you need to confront it, deal with it and resolve it. This does not have to be done alone. Find support from those around you. Get support from a professional if it is a deep personal issue that is troubling you. If you do not deal with it now – it will keep blocking you in different ways throughout your career and life. Once you have worked through the blocks – you will be so much more energised, comfortable, confident and free.

Those are the 10 pieces of the pie that you must do before or as you start your journey and change careers. Each step requires some work, time and thought – but they are important if you really want to make it work. There might be a lot to do – but you are not alone and you CAN do it.

Believe In Yourself!

Landing your perfect job might be tough at times. You may find juggling your time and money brings on stress. You may feel that your family are friends aren't as supportive as you'd hoped. You may find yourself exhausted from time to time or low in spirits. It is very important to stay positive, focused, and motivated.

Do not let yourself be defeated or become hopeless. Give yourself credit for all your efforts, believe in your capabilities and your right to happiness. Try not to let others affect how you feel about the decisions you've made. Give yourself permission to take your life in the direction you want. Keep a clear head, stay organised, and persevere even when the road gets rough!

Ok, onto how to find the perfect job!

**"My mother said to me, "If you become a soldier, you'll be a general, if you become a monk you'll end up as the pope."
Instead, I became a painter and wound up as Picasso."**
Pablo Picasso

Part Two: Finding Job Opportunities

In today's world, we are fortunate to have many options and avenues to explore when we're searching for a new job. We don't just have to rely on newspaper ads or signs in windows. Furthermore there are so many different types of work that there really is something for everyone.

Let's start with the basics you will need to do. Cut down the job search process into easy-to-chew chunks one day at a time:

Write a career plan!
It's much easier to get a job if you know yourself, know exactly where your career is headed, and know what organisation/s you want to work for.

Update Your CV / Resume
Give your basic CV a makeover. Talk to successful friends to find out more about CV writing and make yours snappier.

Personal Brand
What is your personal brand and how would you sell this to a recruiter or employer? Imagine you meet someone in an elevator and you have a very short window to impress them. Prepare a 30 second speech that will sell you ahead of your competitors.

Recruitment Agencies
You know what you want and your Resume is ready. The next step is to show the recruiters that you're a serious candidate. Register with those you've used in the past and research others who recruit in your field.

The Power of Networking
Getting a good job is as much about whom you know as what you know. If there are industry events happening get your butt along. If

not, use your spare time to track down social media networks in your field, join them and start participating in conversations.

Search Every Day!
Use downtime and weekends to see what jobs are out there. Many recruitment websites will allow you to set up email alerts o that you're the first to know when new jobs in your industry are posted.

Actually Apply For A Job!
Ok, so this is the piece of advice that some employers attack me for...but it *is* effective. Consider applying for a job, even if you don't really want it, just to practice the procedure, so you are an expert when it comes to a job you really *do* want!
There's no time like now to write a cover letter and send out your CV. To show your enthusiasm, follow up every CV with a phone call or email requesting a job interview.

Keep Yourself Relevant
If you want to step up to the next level you need to look and sound the part by updating your image. What could you do to come across as more professional, more vibrant, more interesting?

Prepare For Interviews
You can clinch that job providing you prepare. Find out more about the role/company/industry than anyone else and make a checklist of all the reasons you'd be great for this position. Do your research, it really does help.

Practice Makes Perfect!
Ask a friend or colleague to do a mock interview. I find this incredibly effective. Get them to ask you tough and even tougher questions. Keep repeating your answers until you know them off by heart. That way you'll be able to smile and rattle off great answers on interview day.

Preparation Is The Key
PREPARE! It is so important. Without proper and diligent preparation you have zero chance of landing that dream job. Get up

early, bring everything you need with you, plan your route to the interview and arrive relaxed with plenty of time to spare.

Kill The Interview!
Relax, breathe and enjoy. If you have done your homework and preparation you are probably already well ahead of the other interviewees. Smile and be the best that you can.

"He who would learn to fly one day must first learn to stand and walk and run and climb and dance; one cannot fly into flying."
Nietzsche

Job Hunting Tips

The world is very much at our finger tips. Your perfect job is out there waiting for you! This small section will focus on ways you ensure your job hunt is thorough and successful. This list will cover the bare minimums you should be doing on a regular basis and a few ways you can go even further.

Get Friendly With Google

We all know how to conduct a decent internet search for a job. Regardless of where you live, there will be a plethora of large websites advertising jobs in your town and in most cases also in your chosen field. These websites are updated constantly so check these sites regularly.

Earlier when I talked about using your idle time wisely, this is the kind of thing I was talking about. Nowadays you don't have to wait until home time to dial up and get connected to the internet. You can now use your smartphone, tablet, or laptop at any time of the day no matter where you are. There are simply no excuses for not using the tools you've probably got in your pocket or handbag at all times. You can conduct your internet search in a waiting room, on the bus or even while you're in the restroom (if you're that way inclined!). A good idea is to create a specific bookmark folder with your favorite job search sites - bookmark each site and be sure to check daily. Make it part of your routine. Just be committed to using your time to your advantage.

One small tip to keep in mind throughout your search as a whole, but specifically when you find yourself swimming in the depths of the internet: **Stay focused and keep organised!**

It is very easy to get distracted when you're online. You want to read the headlines, you want to know if your team won the match last night, you want to see the latest drunken photos of your friends from last nights party, you want to mindlessly page down a social networking site and let your mind go numb. Set rules for yourself to avoid getting distracted and stick to them. You can set a time limit, or a task list, whatever will keep your mind from straying. Again, I should repeat that finding the dream job is not easy (or else everyone would be doing it) – but it is very possible with the right attitude!

Further, keep yourself organised. Keep records of what jobs you're interested in, what applications or enquiries you've made, what follow-ups you are due to make, etc. to prevent any possible mistakes. Doing this can also be a great way to keep yourself motivated.

Whether you prefer keeping a handwritten list, a spreadsheet, a document on your computer, a list in the "notes" section of your phone, or any other listing method, being able to look over all the work you've put toward your job search can be a great way to pat yourself on the back and a good way to track your progress and reinforce your momentum.

Get Savvy With In-Print Materials

Newspapers and magazines may seem outdated and in some respects they are; however you may be able to effectively utilise in-print materials in your job search. I am not necessarily suggesting you spend a heap of time looking through classified ads in any old newspaper, but, depending on your chosen field, there may be some relevant in-print materials specifically targeted at your interests. You may already subscribe to quarterly journals, monthly magazines, or weekly publications specifying in your area. You might be pleasantly surprised by what you may find in a magazine sitting on your kitchen table right now.

Get Networking

I'm this is not the first time you've heard someone say "It's not what you know, it's who you know". And for good reason! It may seem odd to you at first, especially if you're not used to selling your personal brand, but that is exactly what you have to do. Think of yourself as a product and get selling!

Touch base with any and all people you know who work (or knows someone who works) in your chosen industry. Even if you don't think they can help, spreading the word could make a world of difference to your job hunt. Get in contact with ex-coworkers, past employers, friends, and relatives. Use any and all social events - a get together at a neighbour's house, a charity event, your son's soccer game, anything - as a forum for launching your product (YOU!). It is more than possible that your friend "knows a guy who knows a guy".

Now is not the time to be shy. Spread the word about yourself! You may be surprised how quickly word-of-mouth travels.

Get Recruited

Get yourself registered with a recruitment agency, specialist, or head hunter who specialises in your field of work and who is excited by you and your potential. By doing this you may develop a whole team of people working alongside you on your job search. The advantage of such agencies and specialists is simple: With the right resume, and a solid interview, you could find a recruitment specialist who has the key to your dream job. Make an ally and you might land that perfect job faster than you think.

Get Specific

This is all about targeting the right market. When conducting your internet search, take it one step further. There are job search websites that don't just cover the broad spectrum of job vacancies but rather, specify on one profession. Regardless of your area of expertise, there is most likely a website listing vacancies in your field. Find them and use them. Furthermore, you can "get specific" by going directly to a company's website to see if they are hiring. Most company websites have a "careers" section which will show any job openings or will alternatively provide a direct contact number or email address to send your resume to.

If you have a dream company, or dream role within a company, make yourself known to them. Even if they don't currently have a position to offer you, they may have a similar role to offer you or may keep your resume on file for future vacancies. Remember, if you want someone to buy your product, you've got to actively sell it!

Now it is time to move on to the section which frightens most people and the one factor which people do wrong and miss out on their dream job – getting references!

"Desire! That's the one secret of every man's career. Not education. Not being born with hidden talents. Desire."
Bobby Unser

Part Three: References

Having good references is an integral part of job hunting as it really can make or break you. If your professional record shows that you have been an asset to other companies, you will be that much more likely to land the job you're after. Ideally, what you want are references that focus on specific qualities that you possess which prospective employers will be excited by rather than vague, underwhelming, or mass produced letters of recommendation.

You won't be able to control exactly what your previous employers will say in their reference letters and you may even find that you're not quite sure how to approach a previous employer. Below you will find a list of tips to get your hands on a glowing reference.

Don't Burn Your Bridges!

Staying on good terms with your previous or current employers and co-workers is essential when it comes to both references and networking. Building a good list of references should be looked at as an ongoing process throughout your working life. Try not to wait until you're job hunting to get started on this. When you are leaving a job, resist the urge to storm out of a job you're feeling less than enamoured by.

We have all wanted to make a scene when we're quitting a job. We've and wanted to throw the contents of our desk to the ground and punch someone's lights out, but you're not Jerry Maguire. Let go of your ill feelings and get yourself some allies. Having a bad attitude will only hurt you in the future.

Ask Promptly and Professionally

Once you have handed in your required noticed and worked out your remaining days at the job you are leaving, it's time to ask for references. Ask people whom you know will give you positive and specific references rather that someone who will copy / paste a standard reference that may be underwhelming to your prospective employer.

It may be wiser to ask a supervisor you have worked closely with rather than a head manager who may be too busy to prioritise your reference. Whoever you are asking, be upfront and direct but also be polite and professional. Ask as soon as possible (don't wait until a month after you've left a job!) and choose the best time and way to approach your chosen referee.

Think about whether this person would prefer to be contacted by email, telephone, or in person. Always stick to business hours and try to avoid times when the person may be very busy or stressed out.

Think Outside The Box

If you are struggling with gaining a reference because you don't have a good or close relationship with the head of your company or you feel that person is too busy to approach, don't ask them for this type of favour as it may end up hurting you in the end. Choosing a co-worker or supervisor who can be specific about your work may be an even better candidate for referee.

If you have already burned your bridges, think about who else might be able to attest to your character, your ambitions, your professionalism, or your potential.

The sort of people to ask could include:

* A professor
* Teacher or tutor you once learned from

* Past co-workers or friends you once worked with
* Fellow members of any societies or clubs you may belong to

Think outside the box and don't be shy!

Stay In Contact

Once you have left a job in a professional manner, be sure to keep in contact with your employers and co-workers to make sure they don't forget about you and are still on your side. Furthermore, once someone has agreed to act as referee for you, be sure to contact them when you think they may be contacted by a prospective employer so they are prepared to respond promptly and aren't caught off guard.

Don't Assume

Whatever you do, don't just give out someone's name and number as a reference and hope for the best. Make sure you do actually ask them for their reference so you can be sure they're not only on your side, but also ready for the call.

When To Use Discretion

If you don't want your current boss to know you're looking for a new job, be discreet. Avoid telling the whole office or asking for references from anyone who might reveal your intentions. Ask co-workers or supervisors you are certain will be discreet.

Make It Thorough

When preparing your list of references, include all relevant information about each referee. That includes their job title, any and all methods of contact, and a bit about how you know them and/or in what capacity you worked with them.

"People with clear, written goals, accomplish far more in a shorter period of time than people without them could ever imagine."
Brian Tracy

Part Four: If You Have Limited Experience

If you are starting out in a new field or just starting out in the working world, you might not be sure exactly how to market yourself. Or you may feel concerned about having no references. The reason references and job experience is so important is probably pretty obvious to you. The path to your perfect job may mean gaining some extra training or experience before reaching your ultimate goal.

Think of your employment history as a snowball. It starts off small and as you roll it along it will get bigger and bigger. If you are an undesirable employee, your snow ball will get bigger with things like laziness, poor attitude, not showing up for work, leaving without notice, not turning up for you last shift etc and will make your career path a rough and rocky road.

You want you snow ball to be full of positive things so that each time you are ready to take another step forward, you can do so with ease and support. While you're gaining experience make sure you work hard, be reliable, go above and beyond, be personable, and don't gossip or complain in the work place. Below is a list of things to keep in mind if you are just starting out in the working world.

Be Realistic!

You can be extremely knowledgable, educated, and passionate, but without experience, your job hunt will probably keep leading you to dead ends. Remember that you have to learn to walk before you can run. Accept the fact that you will need to gain experience to reach your ultimate goal and try to do so, gracefully. That might mean working a job you feel you are too good for or you feel is a waste of time; however, if you start your career with arrogance and rudeness, you will have a hard time progressing and and even harder time gaining references.

Remember that everyone has to start somewhere. You can know in your heart that you are only jumping through hoops to get where you want to be, but you don't have to tell everyone you work with all about it. Keep a clear head, keep your standards up, and keep your attitude positive.

Gaining Experience Other Ways

If you are just starting out and you want to gain as much work experience as possible and you want to do it as quickly as possible, think about other things that may be relevant to your dream job that you can get involved in. Think about things that may help to show how positive your attitude is, how you can work on our own initiative, or how ambitious you are.

You can gain experience and references through volunteer work or interning. You can do some part time work in another field or take on some extra training or education.

Ultimately, you want to create a picture of yourself that is desirable to prospective employers. You may find yourself feeling impatient from time to time but keep your mind on the end goal and remind yourself that this is a long game. Play hard and keep at it!

Be Curious and Pay Attention

Throughout your working life you will work with many people you can learn from. Take every opportunity possible to learn more and become better at what you do. Ask questions where possible and pay attention to how others progress (or where they falter). Being curious and proactive in your career progression will ensure a faster rise to the top.

Nobody gets to the top on their own. Believe me. It may seem that people just somehow got lucky and I cannot deny that luck does play a factor – but you must create the luck. You must first put yourself in the position to be lucky. This involves constantly learning, consistently growing and never standing still. Then it all becomes so much more possible and more enjoyable.

Now onto the dreaded resumes!

"When you're following your energy and doing what you want all the time, the distinction between work and play dissolves."

Shakti Gawain

Part Five: Preparing Your Resume (CV)

There are many publications both online and in print that can help you create the best resume for your chosen field of work. Due to the fact that your area of expertise will inform certain preferred resume styles, this section will cover the basics of resume writing and a few top tips.

Your Resume Must Include

1 - Your personal information

2 - Your contact details

3 - Your education and qualifications

4 - Your work experience

5 - Any and all relevant skills or knowledge you have

6 - Your own relevant interests and achievements

7 - Your references

First Impression
* Does the resume look original and not based on a template?
* Is the resume inviting to read, with clear sections and ample white space?
* Does the design look professional rather than like a simple typing job?
* Is a qualifications summary included so the reader immediately knows the applicant's value proposition?
* Is the resume's length and overall appearance appropriate given the career level and objective?

Appearance
* Does the resume provide a visually pleasing, polished presentation?

* Is the font appropriate for the career level and industry?
* Are there design elements such as bullets, bolding and lines to guide readers' eyes through the document and highlight important content?
* Is there a good balance between text and white space?
* Are margins even on all sides?
* Are design elements like spacing and font size used consistently throughout the document?
* If the resume is longer than a page, does the second page contain a heading? Is the page break formatted correctly?

Resume Sections
* Are all resume sections clearly labeled?
* Are sections placed in the best order to highlight the applicant's strongest credentials?
* Is the work history listed in reverse chronological order (most recent job first)?

Career Goal
* Is the career objective included toward the top of the resume in a headline, objective or qualifications summary?
* Is the resume targeted to a specific career goal and not trying to be a one-size-fits-all document?
* If this is a resume for career change, is the current objective clearly stated, along with supporting details showing how past experience is relevant to the new goal?

Accomplishments
* Does the resume include a solid listing of career accomplishments?
* Are accomplishments quantified by using numbers, percentages, dollar amounts or other concrete measures of success?
* Do accomplishment statements begin with strong, varied action verbs?
* Are accomplishments separated from responsibilities?

Relevance
* Is the information relevant to hiring managers' needs?
* Does the resume's content support the career goal?

* Is the resume keyword-rich, packed with appropriate buzzwords and industry acronyms?
* Is applicable additional information, such as awards and affiliations, included, while personal information like marital status, age and nationality unrelated to the job target omitted?

Writing Style
* Is the resume written in an implied first-person voice with personal pronouns, such as I, me and my, avoided?
* Is the content flow logical and easy to understand?
* Is the resume as perfect as possible, with no careless typos or spelling, grammar or syntax errors?

Top Tips

1 - Use clean white paper and a full size envelope. Don't fold or crumple it.

2 - Put your contact information in the top centre area of your resume.

3 - Stick to two pages maximum. Be succinct and direct. Avoid waffling.

4 - Ensure the lay out is clean and well structured.

5 - Tailor your resume specifically to each job you are applying for. Look into all necessary and desired criteria for each job and make sure your resume responds to each of these criterium directly.

6 - Avoid unrelated material. Think of how many resumes get sent in for every job. Be sure yours won't get overlooked by keeping your information relevant. This means creating different resumes for

different jobs. Don't be lazy and expect one generic resume to apply to every job you apply for!

7 - When including hobbies and interests, avoid solo activities. Focus on areas of your life that require team work, initiative, and planing or organisational skills and show how they make you a desirable employee.

8 - Keep your language positive. Use words like "accomplished", "organised", "well-developed", "responsible", etc.

9 - Include any information that makes you look like a good candidate for the job. Include volunteer work, internships, group activities, etc.

10 - Review your resume regularly and be sure to keep it up to date!

"They may forget what you said, but they will never forget how you made them feel."
Carl W. Buechne

Part Six: The Interview

Now that you've gained experience, references, and wrote a killer resume, you have now landed yourself some interviews! You're in the home stretch now! This is not the time to lose steam or get caught up in nerves. Your interview is a chance to leave a lasting impression on your prospective employers. This is your chance to really sell yourself. This section is going to cover everything you need to know to keep your nerves at bay and nail that interview!

Getting Prepared

Before you head in to your interview you'll need to do some research. Research the company, the people behind the company, the values of the company, and any other skills they may be looking for. Brush up on any knowledge you may need to know so you can be confident when answering any questions about it. Think about any questions you may have and write them down so you don't forget to ask on the day.

Think Ahead

In the days before your interview take time to reflect on what you have to offer this company. Think of some things they may ask you and think about some possible answers. Avoid memorising a script! To be fully prepared, reflect on your skills and knowledge and think about specific examples where you have used them. Many times, we think of our skills in too broad a spectrum. Going in to your interview with a list of too broad or generalised skills won't do much for you.

Your new employers will want to hear examples of times you've exhibited great leadership, when you used your own initiative, when you've overcome a difficulty or obstacle, when you've worked well as a team, etc. Also, think about specific times you may have failed and how you corrected a problem or learned from your failures.

Be Fresh

Avoid drinking alcohol the night before an interview and do your best to get a good night's sleep. Have a good breakfast and beware too much caffeine and anything that may make your breath smell bad. Make sure you are freshly showered and well presented. Avoid wearing too much perfume or cologne. Pack an extra shirt if possible so you don't stress out over spilled coffee or accidental make-up / sweat stains.

Be On Time

Being punctual is paramount. Nothing says "I don't care" like arriving twenty minutes late! Plan your journey the night before the interview so you know how you're getting there and leave early so that you don't need to panic in the case of traffic or other unforeseen set backs.

What To Wear

You want to look your best and you want to look professional. Remember, your job interview is not a place to make a statement with your clothing. Ultimately, your clothing should act as a solid professional backdrop to your product (yourself!).

MEN:

* A conservative suit in a solid colour

* A long sleeved white shirt

* A conservative tie

* Dark socks and professional shoes

* A clean, neat hair style

* Little to no jewellery

* A briefcase or portfolio where required

WOMEN:

* A conservative skirt or trouser suit in a solid colour

* A professional blouse

* Understated light coloured tights or hosiery

* Professional shoes

* A neat, professional hair style

* Nicely manicured nails and sparse make-up

* Limited jewellery

* A briefcase or portfolio where required

Top Tip: If in doubt, throw it out. If you think a piece of jewellery is too loud, don't wear it. If you think your heels are too high, don't wear them. If you think your top is too low cut, don't wear it! Remember the aim is to look professional. Save your mini skirts and bare legs for the club. Save your colourful neck tie for your Christmas party. And keep your trainers for the gym.

Last Minute Nerves

You will probably feel nervous before your interview. This is absolutely normal. If you're feeling very anxious, take a little time outside to take some slow deep breaths and try to steady your mind. Slow your thoughts down and remember that these people want to meet you. Think about all the qualities you have that make you perfect for the job.

Visualization is an incredibly powerful tool and it works!
Picture the interview going perfectly and imagine yourself leaving feeling confident to get a sense of empowerment. Really picture the scene, run through it in your mind going well. Repeat this process over and over.

If possible, call a friend or partner and get a little pep talk before you get called in. If you find you are getting hot or sweaty, go to a restroom and dab some cold water behind your ears to cool yourself down quickly.

"If you wish to achieve worthwhile things in your personal and career life, you must become a worthwhile person in your own self-development."
Brian Tracy

Your Demeanour

This is everything you need to do to make a good impression in your interview. Follow these steps closely and that job is yours!

* Enter the room with your head held high.

* Shake hands with all people in the room, make eye contact, and smile.

* Be aware of your posture. Don't slouch or cross your arms.

* Have a good, assertive attitude. Don't act cocky nor meek.

* Be respectful at all times and try to develop a good rapport with the interviewers without acting like a clown!

* Ask for clarity if you didn't hear a question properly or are unsure of the meaning of a question.

* Try not to waffle on or talk about unrelated things.

* Focus on the questions, allow yourself some time to think about your answer and then answer to the best of your ability.

* Be positive and enthusiastic and say what it is about the company that excites you and makes you want to work for them.

* No matter how you feel about how the interview went, be sure to shake hands, thank them for their time, smile, and leave with your head held high.

After The Interview

Try not to dwell on the experience or run through it all over and over in your head. There is nothing you can do afterward to change how it went. Give yourself a pat on the back for giving it your best shot.

Learn from any mistakes you made and then let go of them. If you feel like you've had a bad interview, don't let it ruin your spirits or self confidence. We've all been there. I once went through an entire interview without realising that a button had popped off my blouse and was exposing my bra throughout what I felt at the time was actually my best ever interview.

At the end of the interview I noticed it and was obviously extremely embarrassed. I excused myself, turned away and fixed my shirt the best I could, then shook hands and exited feeling absolutely mortified. But you know what? I got the job anyway.

Following Up

There will be some instances where you will be told there is no need to follow up. You may be given an exact date that you will hear by and in an instance like that, it might be best to just wait it out. If not, however, I suggest sending a polite letter thanking the interviewers for their time. Use the letter to reiterate how interested you are in the company and the opportunity to work for them. Let them know you are looking forward to the next step. Don't be over-bearing. Keep it simple and personable. Be prompt with this thank you note, regardless of if you think it's already "in the bag". Your follow up is a great way to show your continued interest in the job. In certain cases, an email is all it takes, but in the case of a more old fashioned industry, a typed and mailed letter may be more acceptable.

If a few days have passed and you haven't heard anything, it's possible that the interviewers are busy; however, making a quick phone call or sending a brief email to check in should be fine as long you keep the tone positive. Avoid a negative or nagging tone. If there is something specific where you may have faltered in your interview, a follow up email might be an appropriate format for rescuing the situation with an extra resource or reference to clarify what went wrong. Whatever the case, keep it brief, sincere, and positive.

Being Persistent and Bouncing Back

If your interview was unsuccessful and you don't get the job, it is important to stay positive and confident in yourself and your abilities. In order to make the most of your unsuccessful application follow a few key rules:

* Maintain a polite rapport if and when possible. You may have not gotten a job with a certain company but all hope may not be lost.

* Always thank the company for their time and let them know that you'd appreciate them keeping you in mind for any future roles. You may end up getting a call at a later date.

* If you feel it is appropriate and you have established good communication with your interviewers, ask them if they have any advice that you may be able to use in future interviews.

* Reflect on how you can do better next time. Let go of your bad feelings; don't carry them with you to every subsequent interview.

* Approach all interviews with confidence! Nobody wants to employ an unconfident person, no matter how well qualified.

* Go easy on yourself. There's no reason to beat yourself up if you don't get the job. Treat yourself nicely, pick yourself up, dust yourself off, and get back out there and **try again!**

"You can't depend on your eyes when your imagination is out of focus."
Mark Twain

Your Dream Job

Hopefully by now you will realise your dream job is very possible but it does require focus and dedication. Just like anything good in life. Read the below ten steps and perhaps go over them every morning or anytime you feel lost or deflated by the whole process.

Ten Steps To Your Dream Job

1 - Have realistic expectations and make realistic plans.

2 - Put your whole self into your search, don't be lazy and, use your time wisely.

3 - Think of yourself as a product to market and get selling!

4 - Use networking to spread the word about yourself and your intensions.

5 - Keep good relations with people who can offer specific references, don't burn your bridges and keep in contact with your referees.

6 - Play the long game. Don't be impatient. Gain experience in any way you can.

7 - Create a professional looking, job-specific resume.

8 - Be prepared, punctual, and well presented at interviews.

9 - Be polite and follow up.

10 – FOCUS! This is the one step where so many people mess up. Constant focus is the most essential part of this process.

Be persistent and don't give up.

"The belief that you can have a meaningful career is the first step to finding one."
Sean Aiken

To conclude, I hope you have gained some great insight here and are looking forward to taking some steps toward getting the job of your dreams. Before I leave you to it, I'd like to remind you of a few key points to keep in mind on your journey.

The first thing I want you to remember is that with the right attitude, your work life can be anything you want it to be. Remember to value your own quality of life. Make yourself a priority and don't be afraid to take a leap for something you feel could lead to a happier, more successful you. Whether you're just starting out, hoping to further an already well-established career, or jumping into a whole new field entirely like I did, with a strong work ethic and a positive attitude, your dream job is only a few simple steps away.

I am living proof that you do not have to suffer through feelings of job dissatisfaction. I spent 20 years at a job just because I was good at it but I knew I wasn't fulfilling my true potential.

I took a leap, and I landed my dream job and became infinitely happier as a result. You can too!

www.ingramcontent.com/pod-product-compliance
Lightning Source LLC
Chambersburg PA
CBHW070922180526
45168CB00005B/2114